DATE DUE			
JE23'9			
FE10'00			

FOOTBALL

Cass R. Sandak

AN EASY-READ SPORTS BOOK

FRANKLIN WATTS

NEW YORK/LONDON/TORONTO/SYDNEY/1982

FOR MY BROTHER TOM

R.L. 3.2 Spache Revised Formula

Photographs courtesy of:
University of Delaware, Sports Information: p. 1,
8; Kathryn Dudek/Photo News: p. 4, 11, 12, 34;
United Press International: p. 7, 16, 19, 20, 24, 27,
28, 31, 33, 37 right, 38, 40, 41, 44; Monkmeyer Press
Photo Services/Eric L. Brown: p. 15, Hugh Rogers:
p. 23; The Pennsylvania State University, Photo-
graphic Services: 37 left; Culver Pictures: p. 43.

Library of Congress Cataloging in Publication
Data

Sandak, Cass R.
Football.

(An Easy-read sports book)
Includes index.
Summary: An introduction to the history, rules,
positions, and skills of one of the
most popular sports in the United States.
1. Football—Juvenile literature.
[1. Football] I. Title. II. Series.
GV950.7.S26   796.332   81-24073
ISBN 0-531-04376-2   AACR2

CONTENTS

TOUCHDOWN!   5

THE FIELD   6

EQUIPMENT   10

PEOPLE IN THE GAME   13

THE FOUR QUARTERS   14

THE GAME BEGINS   17

OFFENSE   21

DEFENSE   25

ADVANCING THE BALL   26

PUNTING   30

SCORING   32

FOOTBALL SKILLS   35

HOW FOOTBALL BEGAN   42

FOOTBALL FOR EVERYONE   45

WORDS USED IN FOOTBALL   46

INDEX   48

TOUCHDOWN!

Hut One . . . Hut Two . . . Hike!
The center snaps the ball into the hands of the quarterback. The quarterback takes the ball, steps back, and prepares to pass. Members of the opposing team rush forward to try and block the pass. The ball flies into the waiting hands of the right halfback. He tucks the ball under his arm and runs. Members of the opposing team surround him. He breaks free and runs down the field into the end zone. Touchdown!

Scenes like this take place every fall wherever football players gather. They may meet on high school, college, and professional fields. Or they may get together in parks, schoolyards, and sandlots to play football—one of America's favorite sports.

The football season runs from September to January. Most of the games are over before Christmas. Many college "bowl" games are played on New Year's Day. Finally, on a Sunday in January, the championship professional teams from both the American and National Football Conferences meet. They play in the Super Bowl to find out which is the top team in the country.

THE FIELD

Regulation football is played on a level field covered with grass or artificial turf. The field is 300 feet (90 m) long and 160 feet (48 m) wide. At each end of the field is a 30-foot (9-m) end zone.

The football field has white lines all around it. Other lines cross the field every 5 yards (4.5 m). These lines look like a gridiron, a grill for cooking meat. That is why the field is sometimes called a gridiron.

Kickoff at the Orange Bowl

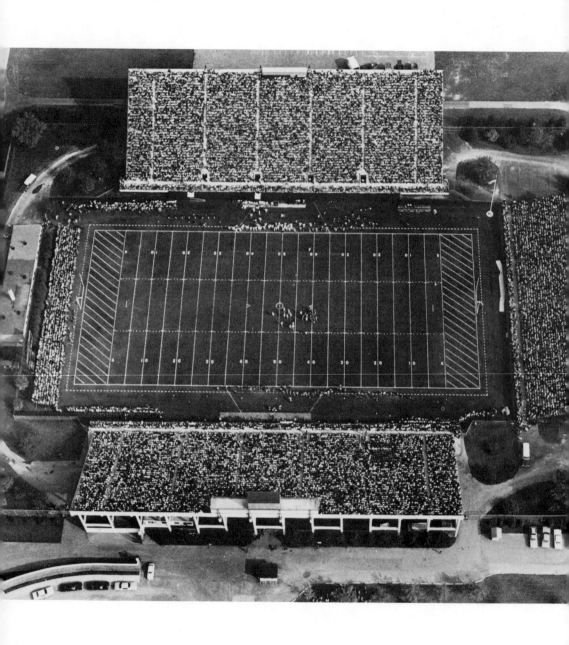

The sidelines show where the playing field stops. Inside the line is the inbounds area. If the ball goes out of bounds during a play, the game stops. The ball is brought back onto the field and placed on one of the inbounds lines. These are two sets of lines that show where the middle part of the field is.

Goalposts stand at each end of the field. The crossbars are 10 feet (3 m) off the ground. The upright posts are set 23 feet 4 inches (7 m) apart on high school and college fields. They are 18 feet 6 inches (5.5 m) apart on professional fields. College and high school goalposts are 20 feet (6 m) high. Professional ones are 30 feet (9 m) high.

An aerial view of a college football field

EQUIPMENT

A football is made from rubber covered with leather. It has four long seams and is laced up the middle. It is oval in shape and weighs 14 to 15 ounces (392 to 420 g). It is 11 to 11¼ inches (27.5 to 28 cm) long and measures about 21 inches (52.5 cm) around the middle.

Football players wear tight, knee-length pants and jerseys with their numbers marked on them. Cloth or plastic pads protect their shoulders, knees, hips, and thighs. Players wear strong plastic helmets with chin and face guards. Many players carry plastic guards in their mouths to protect their teeth.

Football shoes have plastic cleats on the bottom. The cleats dig into the ground and give good footing when the ground is slippery.

Helmets, padded uniforms, and shoes with cleats are part of a footballer's equipment.

PEOPLE IN THE GAME

Football is played by two teams, each with 11 players on the field. Each team has many more players, but only 11 play at one time. One of the team members is the *captain*.

Coaches are the bosses in charge of each team. They train the players and teach them different plays. Often they are ex-football players themselves.

Officials make sure that the teams follow the rules. High school and college teams generally follow the same rules. Professional rules are slightly different.

The *referee* is the most important official. If a player breaks a rule, a referee can give him a *penalty*. Penalties may mean moving the ball backward, losing possession of the ball, or taking a player out of the game. In high school and college games, the referee is the official timekeeper.

**A referee's signal may show
that a rule has been broken.**

THE FOUR QUARTERS

A football game is divided into four periods, or *quarters*. Each quarter in a high school or college game lasts 12 minutes (15 minutes in the pros). Between the first and second and between the third and fourth quarters there is a 2-minute break. Team captains and coaches discuss plans for winning the game. Teams change goals each quarter and move to opposite ends of the field. The team that has the ball at the end of the first or third quarter keeps it for the beginning of the next quarter.

Between the second and third quarters, there is a 20-minute break called half time. In the pros, half time lasts 15 minutes. Cheerleaders and marching bands may put on a colorful show that adds to the fun and excitement.

Cheerleaders entertain the crowd at halftime.

THE GAME BEGINS

Just before the game starts, the team captains meet at the center of the field to toss a coin. The captain who wins the toss chooses which goal his team will defend. Or he decides if his team will kick off the ball or receive the kickoff.

Each team is sometimes on *offense* and sometimes on *defense*. The team that has the ball tries to move it toward the opposing team's goal. This is called offense. The team that does not have the ball tries to stop the other team from scoring. It is on defense. Usually different players on the team play offensive and defensive positions.

The two halves of the game begin with a *kickoff*. The defensive team kicks from its own 40-yard line (35-yard line in the pros). Then the team plunges into the offensive team's territory. The offensive team rushes forward to receive the kick.

Kickoff!

After the kickoff, a football game is a series of separate plays, or *downs*. The team with the ball has four downs in which to move the ball forward at least 10 yards. If they succeed, it is called "making a down." Then they get four more downs to try and move the ball another 10 yards or more. If not, they lose the ball to the other team.

At the start of each down, the two teams line up facing each other along the *line of scrimmage*. This is an imaginary line that passes through the ball and across the field. The location of the line of scrimmage during a play depends on the yard line the ball is on at the start of the play. With each new down, the line of scrimmage shifts to the yard line where the ball was at the end of the last play.

**Two teams head-to-head
on the line of scrimmage**

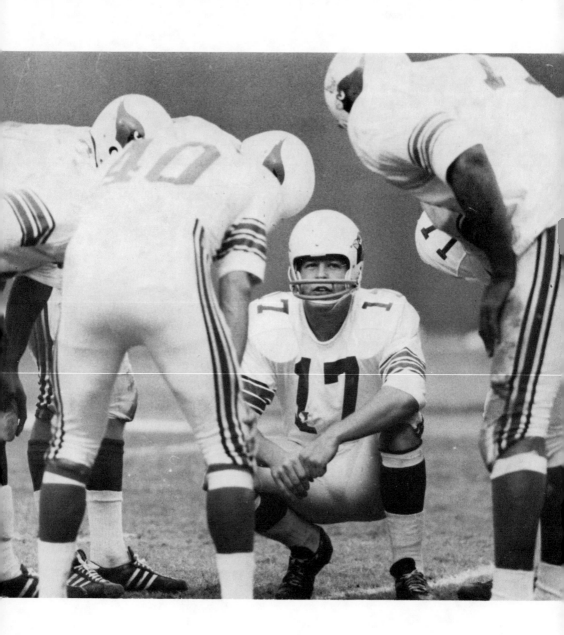

OFFENSE

On the offensive team, seven players are called linemen. The line positions are *center, right,* and *left guards, right* and *left tackles,* and *right* and *left ends.* The four backfield positions are *quarterback, right* and *left halfbacks,* and *fullback.*

In many ways, the quarterback is the team leader. Before each play, he leads the team in a *huddle* to decide on a plan of action. He and his teammates have memorized many different *set plays.* These are careful plans for winning the game. Each player knows exactly where he must go and what he must do. Winning depends upon every team member.

A quarterback leads his team in a huddle.

At the start of each down, the offensive team players line up in a T-formation, or a formation like the T-formation. The seven offensive linemen crouch down behind the line of scrimmage in a three-point stance with one hand on the ground. The quarterback stands directly behind the center.

The center snaps the ball between his legs to the quarterback. The quarterback usually hands the ball off to one of the other offensive backs. They try to gain yardage by running with, kicking, or passing the ball.

The center, guards, and tackles on the front line block players from the defensive team. The ends either block defensive players or run down the field to receive a pass.

The center prepares to snap the ball to the quarterback.

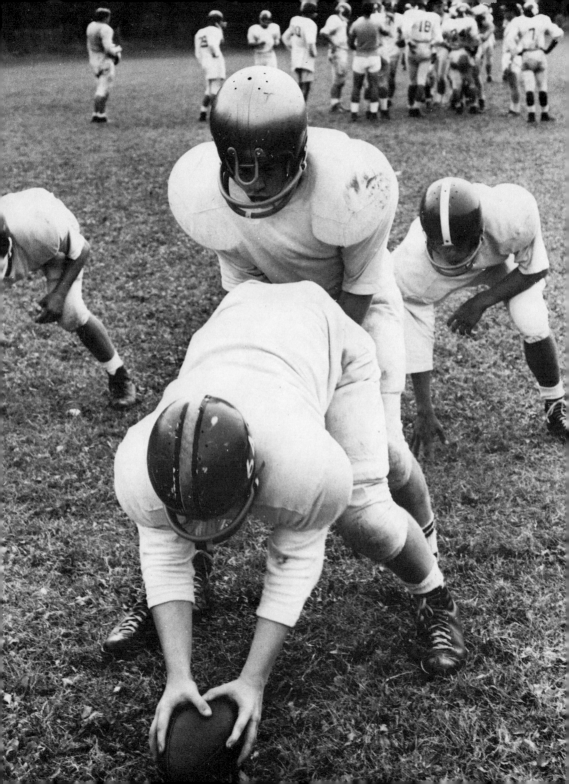

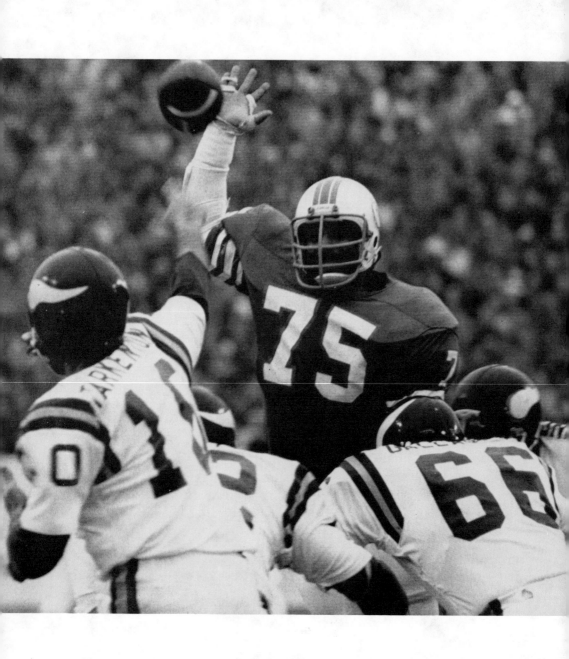

DEFENSE

The defensive team begins each down lined up on the line of scrimmage opposite the offensive team. On defense, all players defend their own goal line. They try to stop the offensive team from moving the ball forward.

Three to seven men stand on the line. Usually the defensive linemen are *tackles* and *ends*. Most pro teams use two big tackles and two big ends called the front four. Behind them stand the *linebackers*. They rush the quarterback to keep him from passing the ball. They try to *intercept* passes and get possession of the ball. They also try to tackle the ball carrier.

Behind the linemen and the linebackers is the defensive backfield. The defensive backs try to stop the ball carrier.

**A defensive player tries
to intercept a pass.**

ADVANCING THE BALL

Good football teams usually advance the ball with plays that combine running and passing. A team can gain many yards with a successful pass. But passing is risky. Passing increases the chances of losing the ball either by an interception or by a *fumble*.

The quarterback must stand behind the line of scrimmage when he makes the pass. Only the two ends or the three running backs may receive a forward pass. If an offensive *receiver* fails to catch the ball, or drops it, the pass is *incomplete*. A defensive player may intercept a pass from the other team while it is still in the air. Then he can run with the ball and try to score a touchdown. His team is now on offense and has four downs to try and gain 10 yards.

Running with the ball is one way to gain yardage.

If a player with the ball drops it or loses hold of it during a play, it is called a fumble. At this point, anyone can take possession of the ball. If the running back or one of his teammates recovers it, play continues as before. If a defensive player gets the ball, play stops. That team goes on offense, and attempts a first down. Professional players can pick up a fumbled ball and run with it. But high school and college teams can only recover the ball and begin a new play.

**A classic
pro football fumble**

PUNTING

If, after three downs, the offensive team has not yet gained 10 yards, it may choose to kick, or *punt*, the ball on the fourth down. If the offensive team punts, the defending team gains possession of the ball and tries to advance with it. It then becomes the offensive team, and the other team tries to stop it.

By punting, the team may be able to move the ball farther back into the opposing team's territory. Then it will be harder for that team to score. A good punt can move the ball 40 yards or more back from the line of scrimmage.

If a punt lands in the receiving team's end zone, the player receiving it can either run with the ball or "down the ball." This is called a *touchback*, and the ball is brought out to the 20-yard line.

A fourth-down punt can sometimes be an advantage.

SCORING

Whichever team scores the most points wins the game. If a team makes a *touchdown*, or carries the ball across the opponent's goal line, it scores 6 points. After a touchdown, the team has a chance to try for 1 or 2 extra points. (In the pros, the team only gets 1 point.) This is called the *conversion attempt*. If a team makes a kick through the goalposts, it gets 1 point. Or it can try for 2 points by moving the ball across the goal line by running with it or passing it from the 3-yard line.

During any one of the downs, the offensive team can try for a *field goal*. This is a kick from the field. If the ball sails between the goalposts, the team scores 3 points.

The defensive team scores a *safety*, or 2 points, when it tackles a player on the opposing team behind his own goal line.

**The referee signals touchdown,
and the crowd goes wild!**

If the time runs out in a high school or
college game and the score is tied, the final
score remains a tie. In pro games, however, a
new period of play, called *overtime*, begins until
one of the teams wins the game.

FOOTBALL SKILLS

Football players spend long hours learning the skills they will need on the field. They are often big, strong men, but football is a game in which speed and skill are as important as strength and size. Many of the best college and pro players have not been big.

Good high school players attract the attention of colleges that have famous football teams. College football scholarships can pay for classes, books, room, and board.

Every football player must learn and practice many skills. These include running with the ball, blocking, tackling, kicking, passing, and receiving.

Coaches give young players experience and training.

Running with the ball

At some point in the game, any player may become the ball carrier, the person running with the ball. The ball carrier should be able to run fast with the football tucked under one arm. He uses his free arm to push tacklers away. Good runners are fast and powerful. They can change directions quickly to dodge oncoming tacklers.

Blocking

Offensive players block by charging forward with their elbows out. A player blocks the opponent's midsection with his head, forearms, and shoulders. Blocking is used to protect the passer and to clear the way for the ball carrier.

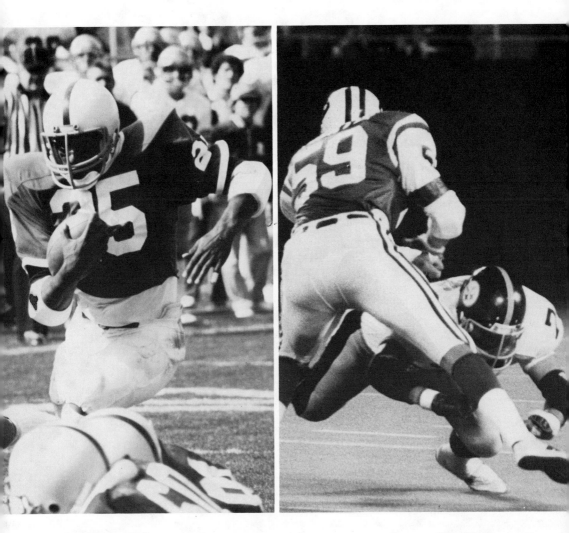

Running   **Blocking**

Tackling

Any defensive player may tackle the ball carrier, but only the ball carrier may be tackled. The tackler rams into the ball carrier with his shoulders and body. Then he closes in on the carrier with his arms and hands to bring him to the ground.

Much of the football played in school gym classes is *touch football*. Tackling is not allowed. Instead, the ball carrier is stopped by being tagged with one or two hands. Players often carry a flag or piece of cloth stuffed in their pants. The player who "touches" them pulls out this piece of cloth to show he has made a "tackle."

Kicking

There are several kinds of kicks. The kickoff is a place-kick made from a fixed position. The ball stands on a tee. Another type of place-kicking is used for field goals or conversion attempts. Usually, a team member holds the ball on the ground with his fingers. Punting is another kind of kicking. The punter drops the ball from his hand, then kicks it before it hits the ground.

Passing

Passes are usually made by the quarterback. The passer grasps the ball toward one end with his fingers spread. He snaps his wrist for a powerful pass. A good pass may go 40 yards down the field.

The pass receiver spreads his fingers with both palms open toward his face. His hands must be flexible or the ball will bounce off them.

HOW FOOTBALL BEGAN

Football began in America, although it is based on much older games. The ancient Greeks played a game in which they kicked a ball across a field. In many parts of the world, football means rugby or soccer. The game of American football is most like the English game of rugby. In rugby, players can carry the ball. In soccer, they cannot.

The first official American football game was played in 1869 in New Jersey between teams from Princeton and Rutgers universities. Organized professional football became popular in the 1920s.

Canadian football is very similar to the American game. Some of the rules and scoring are different. Canadian teams use 12 players instead of 11.

An early football game between Yale and Princeton

FOOTBALL FOR EVERYONE

The greatest names in football are those of men who helped to make the sport what it is today. Walter Camp and Knute Rockne loved playing the sport. They went on to become famous coaches.

Many communities sponsor teams for 9- to 13-year olds. These teams are named after "Pop" Warner, a famous coach.

More than 60 million fans go to football games each year. Millions more watch them on television. More and more people play football all the time. In some places, girls and women have formed teams.

You can play football in a sandlot game with a few friends. Or you can enjoy watching the pros in the Super Bowl. Football is fun for everyone!

WORDS USED IN FOOTBALL

Backfield: The four players—quarterback, right and left halfbacks, and fullback—who make up the backfield. They try to gain yards.

Block: Players block by charging forward with their elbows out.

Conversion attempt: To get extra points after a touchdown, a team may (1) kick the ball through the goalposts for one point, or (2) move the ball across the goal line by running with it or passing it, for 2 points (or 1 in pro ball).

Defense: When a team does not have possession of the ball, and is trying to stop the other team from scoring.

Down: Each play in a football game is a down. The team with the ball has four downs in which to advance the ball 10 yards.

Fumble: When the ball is dropped or a player loses hold of it.

Huddle: A gathering of team members to decide plans of action.

Incomplete pass: If a pass is not caught by a receiver or the receiver drops it, it is incomplete.

Intercept: When a ball is passed from one member of the offensive team toward another but is taken instead by someone on the defensive team, it is intercepted.

Kickoff: A place-kick that marks the beginning of each half of a football game.

Line of scrimmage: An imaginary line on the football field on the yard line where the ball was at the end of the previous play.

Linemen: The seven members of the front line: center, right and left guards, right and left tackles, and right and left ends.

Offense: When a team has the ball and is trying to move it forward toward the opposing team's goal.

Punt: A kick, usually made on a fourth down.

Quarter: Each period in a football game. There are four altogether.

Receiver: The person to whom a football is passed.

Safety: A 2-point score made when the defensive team tackles a player behind his own goal line.

Touchback: When the ball is brought to the 20-yard line after a kick that lands in the receiving team's end zone.

Touchdown: A 6-point score when a team carries the ball across the opponent's goal line.

INDEX

Advancing the ball, 26–28

Backfield, 20, 25
Backs, 5, 9, 20, 21, 22, 25, 26
Blocking, 37

Canadian football, 42
Captain, 13, 17
Center, 5, 10, 21, 22
Conferences, 6
Conversion attempt, 32

Defense, 17, 22, 25
Down, 18

Ends, 25
Equipment, 10

Field, 6–9, 18
Field goal, 32
Formation, 20, 22
Fumble, 26, 29

Goalpost, 8
Guards, 21, 22

Huddle, 21

Inbounds area, 8
Incomplete pass, 26
Interception, 25

Kickoff, 17, 18, 40

Lineman, 22
Line of scrimmage, 8, 18, 22, 25, 26, 30

Offense, 17, 21, 22

Passing, 41
Penalty, 13
Plays, 20
Punting, 30, 40

Rugby, 42
Rules, 13
Running with the ball, 36, 37

Safety, 32
Scoring, 32–33
Sidelines, 8
Skills, 34–40
Super Bowl, 6

Tackles, 21, 22, 25
Tackling, 39
Team, 12
Touchback, 30
Touchdown, 5, 32
Touch football, 39